Contents

Written by
Benjamin Hulme-Cross

Illustrated by
Fabio Leone

Series editor **Dee Reid**

T0351886

ALWAYS LEARNING   **PEARSON**

Before reading The Howling

Characters

Carl

The Captain

The woodcutter

Lady Lupin

New vocabulary

ch1 p5 jeered
ch1 p5 strode
ch2 p8 distract

ch2 p9 murmured
ch2 p11 glared
ch3 p15 bleating

Introduction

My name is Carl and I am a servant to a Captain who fought bravely in the wars. Now the wars were over and the Captain and I were heading home. As we walked through the forest at night I heard the howling of wolves. Then I heard a different sound – a terrible low growl. What creature was out there?

The Howling

Chapter One

The wars were over and the Captain and I were heading home. We had been walking through the forest for hours and I was very tired. The moon was full and through the trees I could see eyes glowing in the shadows. The cold, yellow eyes of wolves. Then the howling began.

"Carl," hissed the Captain, "light the torch." My hands shook as I lit the torch. Then we heard a terrible, low growl and at once the howling stopped.

The glowing yellow eyes had gone. Only two eyes were left. They were big and blue and there, in front of me, stood a massive, silver wolf.

I screamed and grabbed the Captain's arm.

"Look! There!" I gasped. But when the Captain turned to look, the wolf had disappeared.

"You are so weary, your mind is playing tricks on you," jeered the Captain. "There's a village nearby where we can rest."

The Captain strode ahead. He was not afraid of anything. I stumbled on behind him. I sensed those huge blue eyes on me again, but I didn't dare turn around.

Suddenly we heard a deep, growly voice, "What brings you strangers to these woods?"

We spun round. There was a huge man with wild silver hair. In one hand he held an axe.

The Captain reached for his gun but the man shook his head and said, "It's not men you need to fear in this forest, there are much worse dangers."

"Then what are you doing here?" asked the Captain sharply.

"I'm the village woodcutter," said the man lifting up the heavy axe. "I know the dangers. Why are you here?"

"We are returning from the war and we need a

place to sleep," said the Captain.

The woodcutter stared at us with clear blue eyes.

"Go on your way," he grunted.

Chapter Two

We arrived at the village inn.

"We need beds and food, now!" shouted

the Captain.

Two men turned to see who had spoken so rudely.

I thought the Captain would end up in a fight, so

to distract them I quickly said, "There are wolves

out there! Hundreds of them!"

The men glanced at each other. Then one of them

said, "Yes, there are many wolves in the forest."

"And something much worse than a wolf," said the other man.

"What do you mean?" asked the Captain.

"There's one huge evil wolf in the forest," murmured the barmaid.

"It's the size of a horse!" said one man.

"And it doesn't just kill, it tortures its prey first," said another man.

"My brother saw it rip off a goat's head and then swallow its body whole," said the first man.

"IDIOTS!" roared the Captain. "A wolf could not swallow a goat!"

The room fell silent, then the barmaid said quietly, "But a werewolf could."

Just then, someone else spoke. "You are fools to believe those old stories!" Everyone turned to look at the woman who was standing in the doorway.

"Who are you?" demanded the Captain rudely. The woman's eyes filled with anger. "I am Lady Lupin. I own this village. I came to welcome you to my village. But I see now that you are just as rude as these ignorant villagers!"

As Lady Lupin turned to leave she glared back at the Captain. "Do you believe in werewolves?" she asked.

"Of course not!" the Captain replied with a laugh.

"I wish the werewolf would attack her," whispered the barmaid.

I looked out into the darkness and my heart skipped a beat. I saw the woodcutter looking right at me.

Chapter Three

Inside the inn, the Captain was doing a deal.

"How much would you pay if I were to get rid of this werewolf?" he asked.

"Name your price," said one of the men.

Suddenly the door swung open. Something flew through the air and landed with a thump on the floor. The barmaid started to scream. Staring up at us from the floor was the head of a goat. The dark blood was still wet.

"I'll find your werewolf," said the Captain, "but I will need another goat."

"Take whatever you need from the yard," said the landlord.

I tried to explain to the Captain about the woodcutter but he wasn't listening. "You stay here," the Captain snapped at me. Then he set off out into the darkness. I ran to the window and saw him dragging a goat towards the forest.

Then I saw someone following the Captain. It was the woodcutter!

The Captain needed my help. Shaking with fear I stepped out into the night. By the light of the moon I could see the Captain walking along the road tugging at the goat's lead. The woodcutter was a little way behind him. Very quietly, I followed.

But when the Captain and the woodcutter got to the shadows of the wood they both vanished from sight.

I ran forward but there was no sign of them.

I heard the goat bleating and I saw it tied to

a tree as bait for the wolf. The Captain was

probably hiding with his gun, but where was

the woodcutter?

Chapter Four

I crept on. Up ahead I heard that terrible low growl again and the bleating of the goat became more desperate. I turned to run. Then I heard a gunshot. I looked back. The goat was gone but the woodcutter was charging towards me, waving his axe above his head and with a wild look on his face.

Then he threw his axe with all his might. I dropped

to the ground and hid my face in my hands waiting

to die. Next I heard a howl of pain and I felt strong

hands pulling me up. The woodcutter had me in

a tight grip but through the trees I could see the

terrible blue eyes of the huge wolf. It had been

right behind me. The axe was stuck in its shoulder.

The wolf howled again and shook off the axe.

Then it sprang at us. I closed my eyes and held

my breath.

I heard another gunshot and opened my eyes

to see the wolf crashing to the floor. Then the

Captain stepped out from the trees, his gun

pointing at the wolf.

"I warned you of the dangers in this wood,"
said the woodcutter. "I followed you because I
knew the dangers. Your boy followed me because
he thought I was your enemy."

But the Captain wasn't listening. He was staring at
the ground.

I looked down. There was no sign of the wolf.

At our feet lay the lifeless body of Lady Lupin.

She had an axe wound in her shoulder and she

had been shot. It took me a few moments to work

things out. Then I realised that the bright light of

the full moon was shining down on a werewolf.

Quiz

Text comprehension

Literal comprehension
p4 What had frightened the wolves with yellow eyes away?

p9 What do the villagers think is out in the forest?

p13 What does Carl want to explain to the Captain?

Inferential comprehension
p12 Who has thrown the goat's head into the inn?

p14 Why does Carl think the Captain needs his help?

p16 What had happened to the goat?

Personal response
- Do you think the Captain would have gone into the forest if he believed in werewolves?
- Would you have followed the Captain into the forest?
- Why do you think the werewolf was about to attack Carl?

Author's style

p13 Which speech verb shows that the Captain was cross with Carl?

p14 Which phrase does the author use in the second sentence to show how Carl was feeling?

p15 What kind of sentence does the author use at the end of the chapter to build up the tension?

Characters

- Captain (a fearless soldier)
- Barmaid
- Farm Worker
- Blacksmith

Setting the scene

The Captain has stopped at an inn for the night. He has met Lady Lupin, the cruel landowner who the villagers hate. Then they tell him about a huge wolf that is terrorising the village. The Captain thinks they are exaggerating, but when they offer money if he will get rid of the wolf, the Captain is tempted.

Captain: Lady Lupin seems like a nasty person.

Barmaid: She is a very nasty person. She's cruel and selfish.

Farm Worker: Just last month she forced old Tom Carver off his land for missing his rent. Old Tom just could not pay.

Blacksmith: She knew that the harvest was terrible this year. But the rent still went up.

Barmaid: One of these days she will end up with a knife in her back. And no one here will be sorry. She's a monster.

Captain: So why don't you stand up to her?

Blacksmith: If we stand up to her then she will drive us out of our homes. She owns all of the land in the village.

Farm Worker: How would my three year old girl survive the winter out in the woods if we were made homeless? Stand up to Lady Lupin and you die.

Blacksmith: Of course, if there was someone who didn't live on her land...

Barmaid: Someone who was strong and brave...

Farm Worker: If Lady Lupin were to have a nasty accident...

Captain: If you're looking for an assassin, I'm not your man. Even if she is a monster.

Barmaid: Trust us, she's a monster all right.

Captain: Speaking of monsters, you don't really think there's a werewolf out there killing cattle do you?

Blacksmith: *(crossly)* So you think Lady Lupin was right and that we are fools?

Captain: I don't say you're fools. But I've never seen a werewolf. And I've seen a lot in this world.

Barmaid: But you haven't seen anything as scary as what we have seen in the woods.

Farm Worker: We have already told you about the huge wolf with blue eyes.

Captain: So what if there is a huge wolf with blue eyes?

Blacksmith: But it does things a wolf could not do.

Captain: Like what?

Blacksmith: It takes its prey from behind locked gates.

Captain: Wolves are cunning, we know that, especially hungry wolves.

Farm Worker: If it was a hungry wolf, then why doesn't it eat the cattle it takes?

Captain: What do you mean?

Blacksmith: We have found the bodies out in the woods. You wouldn't expect that from a hungry wolf.

Barmaid: Anyway, it's not just cattle that have been taken.

Farm Worker: Sssh! We shouldn't speak of this.

Captain: Go on.

Barmaid: In the last year three babies have been taken. They just disappeared and were never found.

Captain: That doesn't prove there is a werewolf...

Blacksmith: We don't need proof. We live here. We know the werewolf took them.

Barmaid: We need someone to rid us of this werewolf.

Farm Worker: And that person is you!

Captain: Have none of you tried to kill the wolf already?

Farm Worker: Well...

Barmaid: Sssh! No need to scare the Captain!

Captain: What were you saying?

Farm Worker: We hired a hunter to kill the werewolf last year. He went out in the woods one night and never came back. Now nobody leaves the village at night.

Blacksmith: Except for the woodcutter.

Barmaid: That's because he's a fool! He's out in the woods day and night but he says he has never seen the werewolf.

Captain: That's because there is no werewolf!

Farm Worker: Of course, you know we would pay you well.

Captain: What would you pay if I were to rid you of this werewolf?

Blacksmith: Name your price.

Captain: Name my price? Then I'm your man. Your werewolf is as good as dead.

Quiz

Text comprehension

p23 Why won't the villagers stand up to Lady Lupin?

p25-27 What things have happened to make the villagers believe it is no ordinary wolf?

p29 What makes the Captain change his mind?

Vocabulary

p24 Find a word meaning 'killer'.

p26 Find a word meaning 'crafty'.

p27 Find a word meaning 'evidence'.

Before reading *Running with Wolves*

Find out about

- what it is like to be a wolf.

New vocabulary

p32 seeking

p35 instantly

p34 swerve

p38 extinction

Introduction

Wolves are powerful hunters who have excellent sight, hearing and sense of smell. They hunt in packs and can track and kill deer and other prey. There is a pecking order within the pack and each wolf must wait its turn to feast on the prey.

Running with Wolves

Wolf Facts

If you were a wolf, you could:

- break a deer's neck with one snap of your long, sharp teeth
- smell a rat from nearly 2 miles away
- run 50 miles a day, every day
- hear a leaf landing on the ground behind you or a wolf howling 10 miles in front of you
- run twice as fast as the fastest sprinter.

Hunting

If you were a wolf and you were hungry,
you would have to hunt for your food. You
would stand up, arch your back and howl.
One by one the rest of the pack of wolves
would join you. There would be about ten
wolves in your pack. They would howl too.
Then you would all set out, seeking an
animal to kill and eat.

If you were a wolf, you would lift up your head and sniff the air. You might smell a deer far away. Then you would run fast, for miles and miles. The smell of the deer would get stronger. One or two of your brothers and sisters from the pack would run with you, all hunting the same deer.

Wolves follow the deer by smelling the tracks on the ground.

Then you would see the deer running through the grass in front of you. You would sprint forward. As you got close you would leap up at the deer. The deer would swerve out of your reach. Again you would sprint forward. This time you would make no mistake. Your jaws would snap shut around a hind leg of the deer.

The deer would fall to the ground, but in a moment it would be up again, limping away. You and your brothers and sisters would leap up again, tearing at the flesh and bones of the deer. It would sink to the ground. You would open your jaws wide and shut them around the deer's throat, killing it instantly. The blood would taste warm and good.

If you were a wolf, you would throw back your head and howl again, calling the rest of the pack. The father of the pack would eat first. If you ate out of turn, the rest of the pack might turn on you. If that happened, you might have to leave the pack. Even if you were only twelve months old you might have to leave and set up your own pack.

But if you ate when it was your turn you would stay with the pack. When you were all full, you would move on until you were tired. Then you would sleep in a cave or a den. Or if it was warm, you might sleep outside. You would not fear other hunters. If you were a wolf, you would be at the top of the food chain.

Wolves and Humans

Which three creatures kill wolves?

- tigers
- other wolves
- humans

Humans are the biggest threat to wolves. In some countries there are no wolves anymore because people have hunted them. There are no wolves in Great Britain now. They were hunted to extinction.

Why do humans hunt wolves?

- Is it because wolves kill cattle?
- Is it because they fear wolves?

In fact, it is very unusual for a wolf to kill a human. There are even true stories of lost children being brought up in the wild by packs of wolves. In some cases these children grow up thinking that they are wolves. Could this be where the idea of werewolves comes from?

Quiz

Text comprehension

Literal comprehension
p31 What is the evidence that wolves have good hearing?

p32 How do wolves call the pack together?

p36 How does a pack of wolves treat a wolf who eats out of turn?

Inferential comprehension
p32/33 Why do wolves hunt in packs?

p34 What tactics can a deer use when it is being chased by wolves?

p36 Why are there such strict rules about who eats first?

Personal response
- Why do you think so many people are scared of wolves?
- Why do you think some humans hunt wolves?
- Where do you think the idea of werewolves came from?

Non-fiction features

p34/35 List what a wolf does in order to bring down its prey.

p36 Think of a subheading for this page.

p38 How does the text layout help the reader to remember which creatures kill wolves?

Published by Pearson Education Limited, Edinburgh Gate, Harlow, Essex, CM20 2JE.

www.pearsonschoolsandfecolleges.co.uk

Text © Pearson Education Limited 2012

Edited by Ruth Emm
Designed by Tony Richardson and Siu Hang Wong
Original illustrations © Pearson Education Limited 2012
Illustrated by Fabio Leone
Cover design by Siu Hang Wong
Picture research by Melissa Allison
Cover illustration © Pearson Education Limited 2012

The right of Benjamin Hulme-Cross to be identified as author of this work has been asserted by him in accordance with the Copyright, Designs and Patents Act 1988.

First published 2012

2023
16

British Library Cataloguing in Publication Data
A catalogue record for this book is available from the British Library

ISBN 978 0 435 07155 4

Printed in Great Britain by Ashford Colour Press Ltd.

Acknowledgements
The author and publisher would like to thank the following individuals and organisations for permission to reproduce photographs:

(Key: b-bottom; c-centre; l-left; r-right; t-top)

Alamy Images: Alaska Stock 34, Picture Press 35; Getty Images: National Geographic 33, 36-37; iStockphoto: Keith Szafranski 1, 32; Shutterstock.com: S-BELOV 31, Timofey 38

Cover images: Back: Getty Images: National Geographic

All other images © Pearson Education

Every effort has been made to contact copyright holders of material reproduced in this book. Any omissions will be rectified in subsequent printings if notice is given to the publishers.